MW01491461

LOOKING INTO A MIRROR

Geneva Rose

Geneva Rose
January 2016

Copyright © 2017 by Geneva Rose
Cover Art Mary Ellen Rose
Girl Looking Into A Mirror
Magic Marker Drawing
Design and photo by Elizabeth Rose Moses

All rights reserved.

ISBN-13: 978-1519738998
ISBN-10: 1519738994

.

REACHING INTO THE MIRROR

OF MY WORLD

I MELT INTO A POTPOURI OF EXPRESSION

FAMILY - GARDENS

&

NOTICING THINGS

CONTENTS

THERE IS

space between
 a moment, an interval, time to reflect, to contemplate,
 to evaluate, to measure, ponder, deliberate, a lapse,
  or gap, a moment of escape.
 Fall is bounty, vibrant color, glorious skies,
 shedding leaves, hunkering down, letting go,
 carpets of rolled hay, acres of trimmed fields.
 Spring bursts in crocus and daffodils, freshness,
 renewal, promise, dandelions, wet pavements,
  fragrant rains, emerald green
but there was space between.
 Winter is full-orbed sun, glistening ice, mounding
 snow, darkened landscapes, bleak trees, frozen ponds,
 comforts of home, Christmas and Hanukah.
 Summer warms us, shade and sun, gathering clouds
 lightening, thunder, early mornings, fog, star lit nights.
  sleepy August days, on-coming September
but there was space between.
 Ebbing, receding,flowing,turbulence, wonder, who -
 what – when - where - why - how - backward, forward,
 and space between to
  contemplate, evaluate, measure, ponder, deliberate.

December 2013

1

IMAGES

From time to time - set in motion by waft
of fragrance or roused perhaps by rustling
leaves - gray-green undersides showing as
a sudden breeze works itself into a steady
gust - that day of sudden rain - memories.

Singing - I'm always singing - Mal, Bud and
Gen - scores in hand performing with the
university chorus George Frederick Handel's
Messiah - and there you are - we've just
met and started to date.

Here I am at the Detroit Yacht Club - a
sorority welcoming party - October 1945
a little black dress - expectation - I'm only
nineteen.

Snapshots of the mind - not reproductions
from a camera's lens - these are memories
recalled - never faded blurred yellowed with
age or smudged ripped frayed - not captured
on canvas or paper nor drawn with a pencil
or pen - but renewed time and time again.

March 2015

EXULTATE JUBILATE

Sometimes thinking in depth about
aspiration and development
pertaining to oneself the realization
occurs that growth and emergence
happen on the stage of life not in a
vacuum or bubble but in the face of
interaction amongst others.

Transformation from a cocoon to a
butterfly - with wings that flutter and
fly - embracing strength criticism turns
into a learning device and wading
through boos and cheers endurance
becomes enlightened performing.

Ownership gives place to outpouring
sharing - in accomplishment music
dance and art - and color emblazons
the dull and drab with life.

December 2014

"Exultate, Jubilate"
motif for soprano, orchestra and organ
by Wolfgang Amadeus Mozart

FIRST IMPRESSIONS

Reaction!
Immediacy taking effect discernment
and perception spring into action.
Eyes and ears coupled with taste
accentuate accept or reject - feelings
that signal savory or flat chide and
acquiesce in a kind of domino effect.

Second and Third Encounters!
Staid analytical superficiality fades
as a sense of warmth and appreciation
predominates toward the newly found
now quite unrecognizable from that
first encounter.

How different things look when viewed
from this new angle of perspective.

June 2014

THE OPPOSITION

I'm keeping track of things
in my own way - stumbling over
prodding and pushing that won't
quit - square pegs refusing
to fit into comfortable rounds.

This thing is insistent -
a voice not mine is arguably wrestling
it's like two of us here.
Raisins stuff compact agreeable in a
measuring cup and jelly beans
don't care boxed round or square.

Stay territorially rooted stick with the
original plan avoid moving into
never-never-land - the voice says
but life in a rut can be terribly dull
I jump in to say - besides –
evidence supports

that both square pegs and round
fit in a whole -
spelled with a w, please.

May 2015

THERE'S SOFTNESS IN COLOR

A scribbled note falls from my book
New Year resolutions for 2015 it says
think of yourself as an artist sketching
washing a mix of raw umber diluted
with turpentine over a fresh canvas.

Brush poised like a pen strike bold
strokes of significance upon its muted
soft brown surface. It will have circles
that encompass and lines that reach out
to expectancy but there will be curves
sweeping over the whole of it forgiveness.

Things don't stay the way we wish –
sometimes it's something of the moment
that gives stretches bends gives again
makes room for us just as we are yields
accepts accommodates fits - a garment
made of spandex - forgiveness.

April 2015

HOLIDAY POTATOES

We see things differently, of course,
although at times we're on the same page
looking at familiar scripts speaking in
commensurable terms but when a simple
suggestion oscillates sparking controversy
nicety transforms to a territorial stance.

As ruffled feathers flutter to emotional
rebuke bridges submerge into pools of
quagmire. Entrapped compromise drowns
in rhetoric. Could a little elasticity elevate
some of this?, I'm thinking - going over in
my mind the recent grocery store incident.
Perhaps my response was a bit quick.

Wrinkled brow - deep in concentration
she's holding a carton of half and half
in one hand and heavy cream in the
other - which should she chose for her
Thanksgiving mashed potatoes - we're
total strangers our only bond is the
dairy department.

"Some people just use milk," I say
jumping into the thick of it. "Well!",
she huffs, "These are holiday potatoes!"

October 2014

NAWAKAWA ROAD

Momentarily our lives touched.
Residents - three of us at the elevator
two more catch up - our Executive Director
and her young summer intern wearing his
black business suit. Another stands aside
a visiting person muscular husky tattooed
deeply absorbed - IPod in hand - his T-shirt
letter messaged - a navy blue baseball cap
shades his eyes - destination - third floor –
All Seasons.

We are variety - differing states and stages
of it - patience - expectancy - isolation –
some more - some less.

My imagination is starting to assert itself.
Consider us on extended mission agreeing on
a collective approach. Could our dialogue
be significant would it even make a difference
or perhaps we might simply revert to apologues
allegorical moral fables - like the far-flung stories
a group of pilgrims told to amuse themselves on
their way to Canterbury in Geoffrey Chaucer's
Canterbury Tales?

June 2015

LAUNDRY SPEAKS

Acoustics in the laundry pick up like
seeds rattling in a hollow gourd.
Heavy metal zippers buttons buckles
things that make noise exercise in
washing machines thump and bump complaints
confined to dryer drums.

Automation at its best is on attack in
shiny clean hard surface environs.

Motion must be round, I think.

But there is warmth - Anna
gentles folds to her completed load
tenderly strokes each small pile
steadying it to stack a white-wire
handled tall shopping market basket.
Carefully removing lint from the trap
Anna wheels out.

May 2015

RENEWAL

In dark, ominous funnel-like form,
mad-furry wrecked havoc. Hurling
its mangled mass of destruction
before it, the tornado* leveled
devastation to its path.

But in the morning, interrupting
the clouds, sun broke through.
Lifting the tormented area it
dispatched a sunbeam to
transform a broken chunk of
white bottle glass into a jewel
of refracted multi-color - as if
to say, "Start rebuilding today."

Energized - awakened -the
vitalizing activity of humanity
counter-attacked - raising its
hand in community strength
routed rubble - refurbished –
restored.

*Washington, Illinois December 2, 2013

December 2013

SMALL THINGS

give continuity to our days, weeks
months and years - although we do
not often think of them in this way –
these patterns of perpetuity that
keep hold on our calendar steadying
it's expected order.

I think of this today - the first Monday
in September - already Labor Day.
Tomorrow, children will trek back to
school in their new clothes and shoes
start the next semester - kindergarten
for some beginners - just the way we
did - my dad, mother, brothers and I
and our children.

There's a feeling of security in it - holding
hands with comfort - a familiar sameness
in something that worked. We've been
there before experienced continuance in
this habitual thing that acts as a ballast
to our ship afloat amidst the clamoring
cacophony of an ever changing world.

September 2014

PERPETUAL MOTION

Running with sameness on its own tracks
confined in circumference of a round
clear plastic exercise bubble
the gerbil rolls randomly across carpets
bumping into furniture, walls and doors
in a zigzag pattern not really going any place

and we on our treadmills IPods in hand
chasing technologies latest reports
competing in marathons pulling a world
along - or are we moving away from it –
ignoring the lessons history has taught
bumping into furniture, walls and doors
in a zigzag pattern not really going any place.

March 2015

COULD THIS BE WASHINGTON D.C.

Here's the yellow brick road and Scarecrow
he's traveling on foot afraid of a match
wanting a brain - a scarecrow with a brain
you ask forgetting that this is The Emerald
City. Tin Woodman tagging along rejuvenated
by squirts of oil from the can in Dorothy's
hand is in pursuit of a heart - now into the
program you inquire if the heart will be made
of tin - and Cowardly Lion hopes to qualify
for a badge of courage. Dorothy only needs
to find home. The awesome Wizard of Oz
can grant all requests but he is tricky avoiding
them hid in disguises - but amidst fearsome
clanging and banging at last they've reached
his thunderous presence - fireworks exploding
lightening belching smoke their knees shaking
at such a display Toto Dorothy's little dog
with clutched teeth pulls back the folds to
reveal a little red faced man shouting above
the din - "Pay no attention to the man behind
the curtain." - he's vigorously manipulating a
giant noise-making machine. Can we relate
to this - an American fairy tale - or is it?

The Wonderful Wizard of Oz
By L. Frank Baum 1900

February 2014

13

A RANT

The innocence of a child's voice cried out,
"The Emperor is not wearing any clothes !"
They were all aware of this, their eyes
confirmed it, the courtiers, the Emperor
himself, the citizenry watching pageantry
unfold but they'd all been duped by two
rogues who aware of the Emperor's vanity
and passion for clothes passed themselves
off as gifted weavers working with the most
beautiful yarn and threads of gold hovering
over their looms in pretense doing nothing
but letting all know that any who could not
see the lovely fabric being woven were
simpletons unworthy of their position - of
course no one wanted to be placed in such
an unfavorable category so they all looked
admiringly on as the foolish Emperor turned
this way and that in front of his mirror   in
the nonexistent clothes the rogues assured
him were of such fine quality they could not
even be felt. Why do otherwise intelligent
people fall for scams, get rich quick hoaxes,
impossible promises, move in herd instinct
following charismatic leaders? Could our
vulnerability stem from an unwillingness to
take a good look at ourselves?

The Emperor's New Clothes
by Hans Christian Andersen

June 2014

ON CURSORY OBSERVATION

of the seven days of the week without a moment's hesitation, the significance of Friday jumps into mind -THIF - "Thank heavens it's Friday!" that is !

Thursday enjoys similar appreciation because of its close proximity to all of the above - but then Wednesday and Tuesday are more problematic, being wedged as they are between Monday and Friday, requiring due diligence ironing and pressing things out - keeping an eye on the days until THIF.

Saturday is appreciably entrenched in its sturdy position and Sunday which was a day of rest and reflection is now buffeted by kid's soccer games, malls and catching up. Why, one might ask this affection for Friday -THIF?

The answer, of course, lies with Monday the cause of it all - Monday with its demand to "Hit the deck running." - Monday deserving this counterbalance.

January 2014

THE TURN

I'm in the thesaurus flipping through words
stumbling on turn - there are twenty-nine
headings and countless ways of expression:
reverse, transition, remake, turn on, off,
over - this is infinite possibility stuff -
differing, exchanging, replacing - thoughts
linking together gather momentum tumble
like rolling stones to the traffic situation.

They call it a roundabout - source of chagrin
bumps into mind - vehicles converging at
intersections - scrambling for position - lack
of signal light protection - ample occasion
for questionable perspective - opportunity
for startled wide-eyed wrong way expletives.

On the other hand - music is celebration in
composition - grace notes that turn with a
delightful twist embellishing expression –
in poetry turns lend a shift - thoughts move
away to a differing position - and dance
embraces beauty and grace - its rhythmic
turns enhance unlike the discombobulated
traffic roundabout configurations.

February 2015

LIGHT

When morning comes, bits of light
slip through the wooden shutter
slats. Outside, gray variations tug
at me, this cold late November
cloudy day. Dripping trees, pebbles
poking up through melting snow,
I watch the gravel circle drive revert
back to its muted wet brown color.

Summer left too soon, I say this
every year. Fading light then dark
settles in upon December's magical
kaleidoscopic warm glowing blush
but January's brilliant light glistening
ice - a favorite month - is a return
to quietness after the hectic pace of
Halloween through New Year's Eve.

Not darkness, light or little of it,
not changing weather pattern hiatus
but our own perception is the
motivating power.

December 2014

END OF MARCH

Sun angling across the east end of my deck
soaks the gray boards with warmth of color
and hopping about in the midst of it a red
breasted robin energetically chirps his
arrival. Spring, I enthuse, hungering for
every special sign I see appearing.

Enough of pale white - day after day winter
fiercely pelting us with snow. Some areas
accumulating over one hundred inches of
the wet stuff coined the word snow-farms
vacant lots for dumping the excess; in the
East, Midwest and Plains extreme cold while
the Great Lakes recorded record ice depths.

Dodging road crews shoveling hot tar,
damage control for punished pavements,
heady with expectation I'm at Bordine's
Nursery with its welcoming earthy moisture
asking expectantly, "Are they in yet?" those
large circular pots, some rectangular, others
small potted plantings of velvet yellow, blue,
purple, maroon - pansies - to grace my patio
April through June.

March 2015

COUNTERPOINT

One lovely theme plays against another in
nature's eloquent symphony of orchestral
medley - unfolding tranquility and sometimes
resounding energy. It's a pastoral - the doe
camouflaged by shade of a tree grove stands
ever watchful nursing twin fawns and under
the tangled old juniper bush a nest is filled
head to toe with cotton tail bunnies perfectly
cylindrical in form like the cover of a lovely
porcelain dish. Crescendo - Mr. Robin has
successfully wrested a worm from the earth
it dangles his beak but forte erupts as the
noisy brash blue jay decides to bombardier
sparrows enjoying their bird bath then slowly
poco ritard - as my miniscule brown toad
returned for the summer frequents the inner
circle of our wound up garden hose. We're
back to - a tempo - listening to the chubby
chipmunk busily chip chipping on a downed
apricot held between its paws. He's making
a mess extracting the nut. Double forte erupts
as small poodle black curly haired Buffy brings
on the percussion section with reverberating
barks chasing a squirrel up a tree and Champ
our neighbor springer spaniel joins in chorus
with the music of the rhythm of the universe.

June 2014

ITS NATURE

A fluff of white dancing on a gentle summer breeze
for a moment stops bumps against my sleeve
for me to take a second look.
I fascinate upon hair-like fibers -tiny spokes
that reach a precious minute seed.
Then in parachute effect lifted by a breath of air
this small ball of fuzz drifts off to some
unsuspecting place to propagate itself.

Ingenious design each in its own way fashioned
parchment-like bearing plump seeds
winged whirly-birds rain from sugar maples
sprout gutters - twirl into gardens
pop up stubborn stalks with sturdy roots
leaf-flags atop. A fleet of them sail upright
between sprigs of grass until the mower moves
through and puts an end to that.

Squirrel gleaners - sowers - random planters
mother nature's team - digging holes hiding acorns
the oak's prolific seeds. Nuts wrapped in hardy shells
protected - planted - left to vegetate – unearthed
disturbed reveal-the shell burst open nurturing
a budding seed and within that small seed
a tall majestic oak tree dwells.

July 2014

SOMETHING BLUE

is stirring in my hosta garden - bobbing
up and down with little jumps and starts.
Probably a bit of plastic has blown from
the Tringali's garbage truck it's Monday
their usual trash pick-up day.

A plump blue balloon has escaped from
someone's open house or celebration
and is anchored - by its matching-color
long satin ribbon tied tightly to its neck –
laced between the broad green leaves.

I could untangle it and let the balloon
float free - but on the other hand is
this a gift meant for me?

Blueness bumping along behind I march
back to the kitchen and wrap the ribbon
around the back of a chair. Now as I sit
across the table - a round smooth bald
head nods approval for my every move.

February 2014

GLYNDEBOURNE SPRING

They zoom past like missiles on an
extended mission. Intent on nesting,
tripping back and forth time and time
again, they hold in their small beaks
mud, string,tall grasses, whatever it
takes, to make a home for laying
beautiful blue eggs - the robins.

Soon they carry tidbits of worms and
bugs to feed tiny hatchlings.

Today, between the large maples in the
back yard, baby birds flexing their wings
flutter from low branches on one tree to
another learning to fly under tutelage of
a watchful chirping mother.

Soon, I'll see them confident - splashing
about under the spray of my garden hose
wanting to have their turn flapping about
in the perennial garden bird bath - after
the noisy blue jay takes leave of them.

Spring 2015

GLYNDEBOURNE SUMMER

My spring pansy pots are petering out.
Encouraged by late May's promising warmth
and pursued by prospects of vibrant color,
my Bordine's Nursery cart is filled with the
pungent odor of lipstick-red geraniums and
over each side a hanging basket of dragonfly
begonias - pink flowers - shiny green leaves.

Come fall - rampant with growth - these will
break out from their pots and tumble
randomly through their restraining wires.

Yellow marigolds are a favorite but since shade
from the maples took over their sunny spot
hosta are better there. New Guinea impatiens
will fill in nicely around the cement bird bath
and I 'II find space for pots among the yarrow,
daisies, lilies, lavender, bleeding hearts, mums
and purple loosestrife in the perennial garden.

The flowering crab by the circle drive could use
an impatiens basket with trailing ivy and so
could the large maple limb extending toward
the back screen porch. I'll be back - I always am.

May 2014

A SLIP OF MOON

In the evening sky, above my deck,
a sliver of moon peeks out
behind a cloud but then hides
itself behind another.

Caught again, this time easterly,
outside my bedroom window
the half disc of silvery light
stays longer - I'm closing-up
the shutters for the night.

Important things can be like this
illusive - hid - covered up –
yet just waiting to be discovered.

August 2015

ITS FAMILY

The motion detector picks up. As
I walk across the carpet Elizabeth
and Jim's Christmas gift to me - a
Digital Frame - starts to spill out
memories from 1952 to 1974
photo-slides pictures caught of us
by Malcolm's watchful eye behind
the camera.

Love like the wind is something felt
and seen in expression - love of family
dads mothers grandparents aunts and
uncles sisters brothers cousins friends
children with adult arms about them.

In our dressed up clothes we pose;
colorful hair bows and black patient
leather shoes; sailor suits and gingham
dresses; dolls, trucks and toy soldiers;
under Christmas trees and in Halloween
costumes; weddings, graduations,
Little League Baseball and family picnics; with
bagpipes the clarinet and playing piano.

Sidewalks, cars, houses, well-kept lawns;
children holding hands and Easter baskets
and through the large French glass window
panes of our house two small faces peer
out - children - always children and the
sunlight illuming them.

January 2015

CANDLES AND CANDLESTICK

I think of the warmth, ambiance, and color that candles bring to a place. Some are standalones supported by their own chubby girth but others are fashioned to fit enhanced and supported by holders - candlestick choices - brass, porcelain, crystal, sterling silver, pewter, pottery, wood - individual designs that give character to the welcoming glow of lighted wicks.

The Persian motif pair designed with animals, flowers and ivy I brought with me when moving house from Glyndebourne to All Seasons, along with the brass candlestick Carol's Mother gave to me when she was visiting and the small pewter one that has a handle for carrying - something Wee Willie Winkie dressed in his cap and nightgown might carry with a lighted candle finding his way through a darkened house. The sterling silver candelabra, Mal's twenty fifth wedding anniversary gift, I gave to Kris who shares my passion for candles.

J. L. Hudson Company's yearly boxed Colonial candle sale was an awaited event allowing me to take a look at replenishing my candle supply with special thought toward holiday needs - a dozen in a box - sometimes ten inch tapers other times twelve - but the ten were best when used with the candelabra keeping the lighted wicks a safe distance from the dining room chandelier - a sense of elegance embellishing the holiday table.

When the children were growing up, a magazine article I read suggested that having lighted candles on the table at dinner time was conducive to encouraging best behavior - I'm not sure of the effect - but as a candle lover I quickly adopted the idea. The rounded wood maple bedpost top scooped out to hold a candle, that Doris had given me, sometimes centered our round oak kitchen table with a sturdy lighted candle as Malcolm, Kris, Doug, Elizabeth and I gathered eating together discussing school and daily events. I can still hear Doug saying: "Let me tell it!" - Kris had jumped in relating something special that had happened on the bus.

January 2014

SPILT MILK

My three - Kristine, Douglas and Elizabeth
she's the little one in the high chair with
the Tommy Tippy cup - it's any day of the
week - 6125 Glyndebourne Drive - we're
at home for lunch. Their wide-eyed
attention lets me know they're in tune
with my usual plea, "Please, don't spill
your milk",I say - but mop-up occurs.

As the white liquid puddles then slops to
laps - runs down the table splashes to
the floor and any undefended spot -
mumbling and grumbling to myself wet
cloth in hand I attack the offended area
knowing I'll not reach all of the stickiness
something will be decorated in white dots.

I think of myself as usually calm not easily
provoked one who adjust to the unexpected
but honesty compels me to admit my past
history of being unglued by spilt milk -
"You've spilled your milk",I say in distress,
of course we are all aware of this but I feel
the occasion calls for special affirmation.

Happily they've all grown into a friendly group
who can with confidence raise a glass to their
lips and not spill a drop of the contents of it.

November 2013

LOOKING BACK

"Waterman", he calls out, running briskly down the
basement stairs avoiding our boots - pairs neatly stashed
against the steps - "Bye", he's up and closing the side
door left unlocked for coming and going – it's Detroit
1936 – he's the water-meter reader.

A large block of ice - held with tongs - braced over his
shoulder against his heavy dark jacket the iceman
deposits the glistening cube in the zinc lined top
compartment of our oak icebox to drip drip drip down
through the trough to the pan underneath the box
requiring daily emptying - "See you Friday", he says.

Milk bottles rattling signaled his truck coming - rolling
to a stop jumping off carrying case in hand bottles
bumping one another - he strides to the milk chute at the
side entrance of the house - an iron box no self-respecting
house was without - inserted through the brick an
exterior handled door to open and an interior one
accessible from the landing of the basement stair - he
reads the rolled note tucked inside one of the empties
hastens back to the truck for items requested. Ebling
Creamery had horse-drawn milk-wagons in some
neighborhoods.

Knocking at the side door, "Mills Bakery", his pleasant
voice said, - a large wicker basket slung over his arm -
bread - cookies - small cakes - "The date-filled cookies are
on special today" , No kitchen counter was complete
without a decorated tin bread box sitting on top: and
inside the house there's the click click of a Smith Corona
manual typewriter - messy carbon paper needed for
copies - a small round spool with inked ribbon that
comes in a little tin box: taking the telephone receiver
from its cradle lifting it to our ear we hear the operator
say, "Number please, - she's a very instrumental part of
the phoning process: on the radio we listen to The Lone
Ranger. We come and go through it- our side door is the
opening to our world.

May 2014

WORLD WAR II

Our world would never be the same again. It was September 1, 1939 and Adolf Hitler commanded his superior German military forces to the occupation of Poland. The angst, ominous foreboding and apprehension of the adult members of my family hovered like a cloud as they sat anxiously around the radio listening for news from Europe - news of Hitler's aggression toward the Jews - Hitler's inflammatory voice imperialistically crackling over the air waves. I was a junior high school student living with my family in northwest Detroit.

The United States was not as yet involved militarily in the war until December 7, 1941when Japan bombed Pearl Harbor. December 8th the United States declared war on Japan and December 11th Germany, because of its Axis agreement with Japan, declared war upon the United States. September 1939 until VJD (victory over Japan) September 1945 were the formative years of my growing into adulthood.

I hated the war and its devastation. It was so hurtful in high school to read the names in our Cooley Cardinal Newspaper of former students who had been killed in action - but reaching back to reflect upon the impact of that period upon me, I become surprising aware that I felt safe - safe at home, at school; safe in my neighborhood, in the city; safe even when the newspaper carrier sped down our sleepy early morning street shouting: EXTRA - EXTRA – READ ALL ABOUT IT - JAPAN BOMBS PEARL HARBOR.

I must have absorbed a sense of confidence from the prevailing atmosphere of our unification - we were one in purpose working as a team - one in the commitment to defeat a common enemy -tyrannical oppression. The government issued food and fuel rationing coupons. We planted victory gardens, women canned produce. We shared rides, crowded onto buses and streetcars that ran on time. We could depend upon them. Posters warned: LOOSE LIPS MIGHT SINK SHIPS; advised: VICTORY WAITS ON YOUR FINGERS; admonished:

(CONTINUED)

HELP BRING THEM HOME! Save 10% in War Bonds. My best friend Marilyn's mother went to work in a factory building tanks. Marilyn's brother Billy upon high school graduation was drafted into the army. In his letters home Billy would try to give a hint as to where he might be and we would speculate upon it. Actually Billy was probably not sure of it himself. We later learned that his company had been in the South Pacific. My dad was over the draft age and besides he had four children.

My family has a treasure in the extensive Journal my brother Roger Lindland has compiled as a sixty year anniversary commemorating the path our family service men followed during World War II. This path led through Sicily, Southern France and into Germany with General Patch's advancing 7th Army; to LST's carrying ammunition and supplies in the Pacific to Japan; to radar operations to New Guinea and the South Pacific, and as Roger has written: fortunately for all of us they came home physically healthy and by all evidence emotionally able to fully cope with their jobs, attend college, raise fine families and contribute to what we have in an economic marvel.

SOLDIERS AND SAILORS

They were not movie stars or famous athletes, just our flesh and blood.
Each was an idol, or even better, an ideal of young manhood.
Each was a blue star in the window of his home.
Each day's prayer was for his safe return.
Each came back to his job or school, knowing he made a difference.
We won't forget what They meant to us.
Our boys
Arthur Gilbert, Earl Klein, Warren Lapham, Malcolm Rose and Robert Tober
by Roger Kyle Lindland

September 2014

67020574R00044

Made in the USA
Charleston, SC
02 February 2017